Song of the Closing Doors

Song of the Closing Doors

| POEMS |

Patrick Phillips

ALFRED A. KNOPF

NEW YORK

2022

THIS IS A BORZOI BOOK PUBLISHED BY ALFRED A. KNOPF

Copyright © 2022 by Patrick Phillips

All rights reserved. Published in the United States by Alfred A. Knopf, a division of Penguin Random House LLC, New York, and distributed in Canada by Penguin Random House Canada Limited, Toronto.

www.aaknopf.com

Knopf, Borzoi Books, and the colophon are registered trademarks of Penguin Random House LLC.

LIBRARY OF CONGRESS CATALOGING-IN-PUBLICATION DATA
Names: Phillips, Patrick, 1970– author.
Title: Song of the closing doors : poems / Patrick Phillips.
Description: First edition. | New York : Alfred A. Knopf, 2022. | "This is a Borzoi book"—Title page verso. |
Identifiers: LCCN 2021045399 (print) |
LCCN 2021045400 (ebook) | ISBN 9780593321423 (hardcover) |
ISBN 9780593321430 (ebook) Subjects: LCGFT: Poetry.
Classification: LCC PS3616.H465 S66 2022 (print) |
LCC PS3616.H465 (ebook) | DDC 811/.6—dc23
LC record available at https://lccn.loc.gov/2021045399
LC ebook record available at https://lccn.loc.gov/2021045400

Jacket photograph by Benjamin Hauschild / EyeEm / Getty Images
Jacket design by Janet Hansen

Manufactured in Canada

First Edition

for Plumly, for Otremba

Contents

Old Song | 3

I

Instead of a Poem | 7
Drink Now | 9
For Paul | 12
The Leash | 13
Elegy with Table Saw & Cobwebs | 14
Meditation at Toccoa Falls | 16
Run It Back | 18
Summer Celestial | 20

II

Song of Suburbia | 23
The Atlanta Hawks | 25
The Couple | 27
The Diarist | 29
On Three Hours' Sleep | 30
Having a Fight with You | 33

Emptiness | 34

The Anniversary | 35

Still Life | 36

III

Jubilate Civitas | 39

Song of the Closing Doors | 42

Chicken Shit | 43

A Treason | 46

A Curse | 47

Palimpsest | 48

May the Living | 51

Prayer | 52

Acknowledgments | 55

Song of the Closing Doors

Old Song

Praised be friends. Praise enemies.
Praise the dark above.

Praise hangovers. Praise cigarettes.
The vulture and the dove.

Praise all music. Praise the harp.
And the amplifier's buzz.

Praise the days we'd live forever.
And loneliness. And love.

Praise even death, or at least the dying,
who taught us how to live.

Praise you, someday, reading this.
Praise light. Praise the wind.

I

Instead of a Poem

I wish this was
just you and me watching
a whole field flare up

in the honey-gold light
of late August—
just the two of us

out on that big rock
covered with lichen
at the edge of the woods,

passing a smoke
back and forth
and listening to the same

noisy quarrel of sparrows
rising and banking
against the late clouds

as a green tractor
drones in the distance,
dropping perfect

little ingots of hay
one by one
in its wake,

until finally the sun
sinks so low—
behind the pink

and then blue
and then almost black
trunks of the birches—

that when I look back
I can't seem
to make out your face,

though even
in the dark
I can tell that you're smiling

and somehow not saying
all the same things
I don't say.

Drink Now

The oncologist says
my friend Paul

will need a total
gastrectomy *if he's lucky*—

Paul the most kind of us,
Paul the most eloquent

lover of food and drink
I've ever known,

who taught me about Barolo
and Barbaresco,

about Burgundian Pinot
and the sunbaked clay soil

of the Côte-Rôtie—
and who will die now at forty

or else survive as never
again the same Paul

once the endoscope
has snaked down his throat,

once the surgeons
have cut out his stomach

and sectioned his esophagus,
and sutured it back

to whatever is left
of the small intestine—I'm sorry

if you're still reading this,
but there's no happy ending,

no plot-twist in which
he "fights it" and "beats it"

and "wins"—
sorry, whoever you are,

in whatever future
you've found us,

but Paul and I also
once lived—

once gossiped and boozed
and so loved the world

that we, too, were almost convinced
it might last without end:

our eyes shining
just like yours,

like delirious kids,
when we used to laugh

into the glorious,
now and forever,

lost eyes
of our beautiful friends.

For Paul

I can see you through the bonfire, with us.
A fifth of Old Crow circling the dark.

Where did that whole life go? In Texas
the chemo inches toward your heart,

things always dwindling to just the two of us,
a crumpled cigarette, a distant car:

our voices, at dawn, so clearly posthumous.
Woodsmoke rising to the ashy stars.

The Leash

When my sister discovered
in a raincoat pocket
the loved dog's long
forgotten leash,

she mocked her tears,
though I will not.
Death is a god
damned thief.

Elegy with Table Saw & Cobwebs

Rummaging the wood-rack
I pull a cracked

old shingle off the stack:
a scrap

on which at
some point, with his flat

knife-whittled pencil,
my old friend Ollie scratched

$5/32 + \frac{1}{2}$—
a kind of riddle now, a workman's

artifact,
unnoticed since that

year the cancer cells attacked—
since whatever it

once meant,
whatever part it

played in some project,
went with him

into the flames
& ash.

Friends,
we die like that:

the whole starry sky goes black
while these little

nothings last—
while these spiders in the rafters

go on clutching
their white sacks:

whispering & yet & yet
& yet & yet

until I dust the fading rune
& put it back.

Meditation at Toccoa Falls

The Irish poet
Patrick Kavanagh
once rhymed
weather with *father*—

just like my friend
Ortiz once called
Vicks VapoRub
bi-ba-poru,

or like the smokers
whose term *hashish,*
over centuries,
became *assassin.*

It's true:
some words
are elegy
to what they signify,

but others
summon the dead
exactly
as they spoke,

like grainy voices
on a gramophone
that plays
inside our throats.

Run It Back

Though he's been gone
for thirty years,
Lou Langston's voice
comes back to me

every time
I stop and stare
at that caged-in court
on West 4th Street,

where tonight the dudes
are talking shit
at this little guard
who slaps his chest

and says *mybadmybad*
just like Lou did,
with a little tap
upside the head

whenever he'd drop a pass,
or miss a three,
or lose the cutter
coming off a screen—

so that for an instant,
through the crowd, I see
my friend again
at seventeen:

still unravaged
by the chemo,
and the wheelchair,
and the shunt,

as he struts out past
some losing team,
calling *nextgotnext
whowantstorun?*—

in that year when all
we ever did was play
as old men laced
their fingers through the fence,

staring like
they knew someday
I'd be standing here,
thinking this.

Summer Celestial

This would've been late '40s, early '50s maybe, when
the boy and his father took a fishing trip

to Canada—where at nine or ten, in a little johnboat
tethered to a hundred-foot-long rope,

he was allowed to drift out on the evening lake alone:
the flaking wood against his back still warm

as the wavelap and the calling loons,
pink streaks of cloud and the first faint sliver of a moon

swelled in him—immense and ancient
and sublime, though half a life would pass

before he even tried to name that feeling
that always began and ended like a dream:

the wet rope creaking, solid as an oar
that slowly, hand-over-hand, ferried him ashore.

II

Song of Suburbia

Always our father
came home to his litter

of wet-haired,
sweet-smelling children,

every pot set to simmer
in time with his whiskey,

ever after as it was
at the beginning:

in that ancient September
of nineteen fifty-nine

when, almost in sight
of the high school,

my luminous mother
first mooned in a window—

first watched
as the interstate's high-beams

flared in a cut glass
and scattered her shadow

up the spattered white
wall she'd scrubbed clean.

The Atlanta Hawks

There was the squeak of the sneakers
and the pulse of the Moog.

Those denim-clad swaggering
dudes with their beers.

Kids Night and Cup Night
and Autographed Posters.

My big brother breathing *you
fuckhead* in my ear.

Rollins to Roundfield
to McMillen to Criss:

our father's black sideburns,
our mother's lipstick.

There was me: half-asleep
at the buzzer, half-dreaming

that winter dark stagger
through acres of cars.

The stars and the stars
and the stars out the window

when I'd wake in a tangle
by my sister and whisper

How far? to the pipe-smoke,
to the dashglow *How far?*

How far? to that endless
lost time, when my mother

still turned like she turns now,
an angel, forever,

to kiss me and whisper
through the darkness *Not far*.

The Couple

Beached on loose-
strapped lounge chairs,

as the sun goes down
they gripe and bitch

in little snatches that I
half-catch on the wind:

something about "the *fucking*
dinner reservation,"

something about "the *keys!*
the goddamned *keys!*"—

their clipped attacks
and insinuations

like those anemones
I saw once, on tv:

who kill and maim
and devour each other

with a stately, glacier-
paced brutality,

just like these two,
who smile through

a haze of Camel Lights
and daiquiris—

love, real love,
a thing they surely

glimpsed once, too,
as it sank slowly

to the bottom of the sea.

The Diarist

It's one long list
of births and deaths,
baptisms and christenings,
who married who,
and where, and when—

all fading into
the ornate script
of a century so distant
it seems less real
than this one

until I reach *Novembre,*
Sixteen Forty Five,
where she left no trace
for eighteen days

then *Peter, a son.*
He did not thrive.

On Three Hours' Sleep

Remember when we used
to do this all the time?

The darkness ripped apart
with babies crying:

babies hot with piss,
or shit, or spewing barf

onto our shoulders
as we paced and sang

and rocked our writhing
little pupas back to sleep,

exhaustion pooling
in our bodies like a drug

that made us late
for everything—made us

gasp awake some days
behind the wheel,

back when we dozed
in subway cars and HR meetings

and slumped on benches
in the kiddie park,

where all the sweaty,
shrieking toddlers seemed

to run on solar power,
or enriched plutonium,

or a pure and simple
restedness we thought

we'd never feel again:
as night after night

we rose like knocked-down
boxers from our bed

to do the ancient, unsung
dirty-work, on which

the survival of
humanity depends.

Having a Fight with You

is like being burned up
in a twelfth-floor elevator.
Or drowned in a flipped SUV.

It's like waking with scalpels
arrayed on my chest.
Like being banished to 1983.

Having a fight with you
is never, ever less horrid: that whisper
that says *you never loved me—*

my heart a stalled engine
out the little square window.
Your eyes a white-capped black sea.

Emptiness

How many cups of tears
that year
when O was dying?

How many little stars
bobbing in hot cocoa
after all those snow days

in the great fluorescent park?
And now: our red-faced
sledders grown,

their dream house gone
almost insufferably calm
when I lean into the hall

and call your name—
not knowing what
it means, love,

to set the hissing kettle
back down on its
burner with a clang.

The Anniversary

At the stainless bar
bros clack their beers.

Thin women stroke
their necks and laugh.

What the fuck
are we doing here?

No one sees us
long enough to ask.

And yet a thousand years
I've watched the way

that loose strand slips
and hides your face.

How do I love you,
in the candle, so?

You know. You know
I know you know.

Still Life

The tabby cat, on the sofa back,
surveys his demesne:
camouflaged in cactuses,
appalled by last night's rain.

My wife lies down beside him,
hair heaped above her freckled neck.
And while I do know—
I do know that the dead

once lived in these same rooms,
once stood here where I stand—
some days are simply good, pure good.
As if we'll always be alright.

Some days your love and the cat curl up
and sleep in the dusty light.

III

Jubilate Civitas

I will consider a slice of pizza.

For rare among pleasures in Gotham, it is both
    exquisite and blessedly cheap.

For its warmth is embracing, its smell the
    quintessence of hope.

For it can be found in all boroughs, every few blocks,
    yet never two slices the same.

For its makers speak many tongues.

For dusting the counter with cornmeal and flour,
    without looking down, they pummel and roll out
    the dough.

For they heap out the still-steaming sauce and, with a
    touch of the ladle, paint it in rings like a bull's-eye,
    or a tree-stump, or a thumb.

For they smile at each other's jokes, grasping great
    handfuls of cheese.

For wiping both hands on an apron, they nod at the
   phrase "not too hot," and start one of a hundred
   little clocks in their heads.

For their corded forearms reach deep in the oven with
   a long-handled paddle, giving each pie, with a flick,
   its requisite spin.

For heat bubbles and blister and browns the
   miraculous crust.

For even in the tiniest shop you can find every style:
   sagging with mushrooms and bacon, broccoli and
   pineapple, chicken, and sausage, and onion.

For time passes slowly awaiting a slice, and reminds us
   how sweet it is to be alive at this moment on earth.

For it slides to a stop in a little city of shakers, where
   with pepper and oregano, garlic and parmesan, we
   citizens make it our own.

For you can fold it in half like a taco and eat it while
   standing or driving, or walking and working your
   phone.

For I have seen the bearded young men of Brooklyn
    sit upright to eat it, riding bicycles through
    redlights, at midnight, in the rain.

For with each bite the paper plate grows more
    translucent with grease, till it glows like stained
    glass over the trash can.

For it has nourished our children and soothed many
    sorrows.

For in a time of deceit it is honest and upright,
    steadfast and good—beloved and modest and
    known.

For its commerce makes nobody rich and nobody
    poor.

For that, to us, it is home.

Song of the Closing Doors

There's a man on the train
nobody sees,
all the way from Penn Station to Brooklyn,

who watches me not-watch,
like an actor pretending,
as he rakes his bald scalp with a comb,

each angry flick
so precisely the same
little flecks of blood pepper his wrist

when the eighth time, every time,
he pockets the comb
and bends down to inspect his toenails—

a gesture so private,
so plainly familiar,
that just for an instant he's real:

his towering church
baritone tolling, *Y'all don't*
understand yet, but you will.

Chicken Shit

I don't mean the idea
but the actual
load of it

that Billy Madsen
used to haul out
in a rusty bin

behind his tractor:
its rotor-arm
broadcasting

a hail of putridness
that greened the fields
that fed the cattle

and every April drifted
down the ridgeline
in a cloud

that filled my mother's kitchen
with a thousand
thousand hues of shit—

all this back
forty years ago,
before the kids sold out

to a conglomerate
that builds golf courses
for the ultra-rich,

whose gleaming Teslas
and black Benzes,
every weekend, tick

in a parking lot
where Bill once kept
his hogpen—

hardly a trace of him
left on the land
but a few stray strands

of stubborn fescue
spiking up between
the bentgrass and Bermuda

that's tended now by men
just as tough
and tireless as Bill was

but in Spanish,
as they steer whole fleets
of new John Deeres

out across the emerald grass
that's pumped
with so much nitrogen

it taints the aquifer
and wrecks the planet
but keeps the putting greens

immaculate
for all the annual
dues-paying Members—

whose whiff of cash
and vested stock
always snaps the laughing

valets to attention—not
because they like the smell
but because

they've lived so long
with the plain, godawful
stink of it.

A Treason

At eighty-two he doesn't visit,
rests mid-stair, forgets mid-sentence,

time a treason all the more outrageous
for having been a man beloved:

who railed, and raged, and gave commands,
yet sits now, mute, while young fools stand—

his good eye's same old, sovereign squint
the only sign that deep within

there lives deposed, dethroned, none other
than his royal majesty the king, my father.

A Curse

When the last of your friends
not dead begin dying

and every window in the brain's
dark cathedral

is lit by the flames,
may you read this alone

in some hip coffee shop,
or packed subway car,

or at the deafening bar
of a starred restaurant,

the names of old loves
a faint tremor on your tongue,

drowned by the laughter
of the beautiful young.

Palimpsest

Because of the rise of Islam
and the depth of the gorge
where Saint Catherine's hides
in the shadow of Sinai,

and because the end of the Crusades
meant an ever-dwindling
trickle of pilgrims
and no vellum for centuries—

and because by 800 A.D.
there was nobody left
in the whole monastery
who could read the oldest poems

and treatises and cures—
no one expected
the digital cameras
and half-million-dollar scanners

to find, beneath an ancient text,
the invisible traces
of a far more ancient text,
that five hundred years before

some apprentice had scrubbed
with lemon and ashes,
his knife-edge clearing the page
for a new exegesis—

so that, as the tiny fan blades
of a black computer whirred,
layer upon layer
of faint impressions in the leather

were illuminated by every
color in the spectrum,
then stitched back into words
that one of the Brothers had written

fifteen hundred years before
in a language called
Caucasian Albanian,
which survives now

in a single fragment
that the project linguist
was able to decipher:
eyes wide, pulse racing

when at last she understood,
via a cognate Udi text,
and whispered "*Net,*
like fishing net"

at her reflection
in a glossy screen,
deep inside Saint Catherine's
Sacred Monastery

of the God-trodden Mount Sinai,
where all of this happened
late in the second decade
of the twenty-first century.

May the Living

who read this
still speak of the dead
with wild imprecision:

sins all forgotten,
rage overwritten,
as even our bitterest

enemies shed
great crocodile tears
and pretend.

I hereby forgive
all the bullshit
that follows a death.

If you're reading this,
we were once friends.

Prayer

It turns out those buttons
at all the crosswalks in Brooklyn
don't do a goddamned thing anymore:

the dead wires hidden
deep in their lamp-posts
all capped and corroded decades ago.

And yet, just this morning,
waiting to cross
in a herd of commuters, by the ice-blackened road,

I could hear that old *click*
click-click as we shivered
and squinted out into the snow.

Acknowledgments

Many thanks to the editors of the following publications, where these poems first appeared:

The Academy of American Poets Poem-a-Day: "Having a Fight with You"

The Adroit Journal: "The Leash," "Mediation at Toccoa Falls," and "Song of the Closing Doors"

The American Poetry Review: "Prayer," "Jubilate Civitas," "The Anniversary," "For Paul," "Chicken Shit," and "Emptiness"

The Best American Poetry 2021: "Elegy with Table Saw & Cobwebs"

The Cortland Review: "The Atlanta Hawks"

The Georgia Review: "Song of Suburbia," "On Three Hours' Sleep," and "The Couple"

The Kenyon Review: "Summer Celestial," "Drink Now," and "A Curse"

The National: "Instead of a Poem" and "Run It Back"

New England Review: "Palimpsest" and "Elegy with Table Saw & Cobwebs"

Ploughshares: "The Diarist"

Poetry Daily: "For Paul"

*Together in a Sudden Strangeness: American Poets Respond to the
Pandemic* (Alfred A. Knopf): "Still Life"

The Virginia Quarterly Review: "Old Song"

Deep gratitude to all the friends and fellow writers whose
kindness sustains me. Special thanks to: Ellen Brazier,
Michael Collier, Brian Komei Dempster, Deborah Garri-
son, Ted Genoways, Jennifer Grotz, Neil Levi, Cam Phillips,
Sid Phillips, Todd Portnowitz, Hirsh Sawhney, Alan Sha-
piro, Tom Sleigh, Tiphanie Yanique, and Courtney Zoffness.

Patrick Phillips is the author of three previous poetry collections, including *Elegy for a Broken Machine,* which was a finalist for the National Book Award, and *Chattahoochee,* winner of the Kate Tufts Discovery Award. His first work of nonfiction, *Blood at the Root: A Racial Cleansing in America,* won the American Book Award and was a finalist for the ALA Carnegie Medal and the PEN/John Kenneth Galbraith Award. Among Phillips's other honors are Guggenheim and NEA Fellowships, a Pushcart Prize, and the Lyric Poetry Award from the Poetry Society of America. He lives in San Francisco and teaches at Stanford University.

A NOTE ON THE TYPE

The text of this book was set in Requiem, a typeface
designed by Jonathan Hoefler (born 1970) and released
in the late 1990s by the Hoefler Type Foundry. It was
derived from a set of inscriptional capitals appearing in
Ludovico Vicentino degli Arrighi's 1523 writing manual,
Il Modo di Temperare le Penne. A master scribe, Arrighi is
remembered as an exemplar of the chancery italic, a style
revived in Requiem Italic.

Composed by North Market Street Graphics
Lancaster, Pennsylvania

Printed and bound by Friesens
Altona, Manitoba

Book design by Pei Loi Koay